LIGHTNING BOLT BOOKS™

The Supersmart Octopus

Mari Schuh

Lerner Publications ◆ Minneapolis

To Fairmont Elementary School

Lerner Publications Company
A division of Lerner Publishing Group, Inc.
241 First Avenue North
Minneapolis, MN 55401 USA

For reading levels and more information, look up this title at www.lernerbooks.com.

Library of Congress Cataloging-in-Publication Data

Names: Schuh, Mari C., 1975- author.
Title: The supersmart octopus / Mari Schuh.
Description: Minneapolis : Lerner Publications, 2018. | Series: Lightning bolt books. Supersmart
    animals | Includes bibliographical references and index.
Identifiers: LCCN 2017044070 (print) | LCCN 2017046068 (ebook) | ISBN 9781541525320 (eb
    pdf) | ISBN 9781541519800 (lb : alk. paper) | ISBN 9781541527638 (pb : alk. paper)
Subjects: LCSH: Octopuses—Behavior—Juvenile literature. | Octopuses—Psychology—Juvenile
    literature.
Classification: LCC QL430.3.O2 (ebook) | LCC QL430.3.O2 S383 2018 (print) | DDC 594/.56—
    dc23

LC record available at https://lccn.loc.gov/2017044070

Manufactured in the United States of America
1-44316-34562-12/15/2017

Table of Contents

Meet the Octopus

An octopus digs up coconut shells that washed into the sea and got buried in the ocean floor. It will use the shells to build a shelter.

Octopuses live in oceans around the world. Most octopuses live near the ocean floor. Others swim in deep water or near the water's surface.

Octopuses search the ocean for crabs, shrimp, and lobsters to eat.

Smart Octopuses

Octopuses gather rocks on the ocean floor. They use the rocks to build homes, much like they use shells. They even pile up rocks to make doors for their homes!

Octopuses shoot water from their siphons to clean their homes. They spray water to push away rocks and junk.

A siphon is a tubelike body part.

Some octopuses hide
in empty shells to stay
safe. The hard shells
protect their soft bodies.
Octopuses sometimes
carry the shells with them.

Octopuses can change how they look to hide from predators. They can change their color, texture, and shape.

Octopuses sometimes shoot ink to keep predators away.

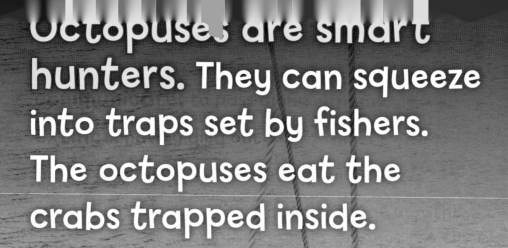

Octopuses are smart hunters. They can squeeze into traps set by fishers. The octopuses eat the crabs trapped inside.

Fishers set traps like this to catch crabs.

Octopuses are curious and will examine objects they find.

Octopuses have learned to do some things that people do. Scientists have seen octopuses open jars, find their way through mazes, and open locks.

The Life of an Octopus

About three hundred kinds of octopuses live in the world's oceans. Octopuses can be many sizes. Some are only 2 inches (5 cm) long. Others can grow to be about 18 feet (5.4 m) long.

Female octopuses mate only once. Females may lay thousands of eggs. They protect and clean the eggs until they hatch.

Young octopuses will hatch from these tiny eggs.

After hatching, young octopuses often float in the ocean for several weeks. Then they settle on the sandy ocean floor. Young octopuses grow quickly.

Octopuses usually live alone. Many live only one or two years. But some octopuses live for five years. Males die after they mate. Females die soon after their eggs hatch.

Octopuses are solitary animals, or animals that live by themselves.

Dangers for the Octopus

Life in the ocean can be dangerous for young octopuses. Sharks, dolphins, seals, and sea otters try to eat them.

Sharks are predators of octopuses.

Octopuses face other dangers too. People in some countries eat octopuses. Pollution in the ocean can harm octopuses.

Polluted oceans can hurt ocean animals of all kinds.

No one knows how many octopuses exist. But scientists don't think octopuses are in danger of dying out. They can adjust to changes in the ocean. They also lay many eggs. This helps keep the number of octopuses from dropping.

Octopuses are adaptable, or able to adjust to change.

Some seafood is octopus safe, meaning fishers didn't accidentally catch or harm octopuses while fishing.

People help keep octopuses safe. They buy octopus-safe seafood. They work to make oceans cleaner. Keeping trash out of oceans helps keep octopuses healthy and strong.

Octopus Diagram

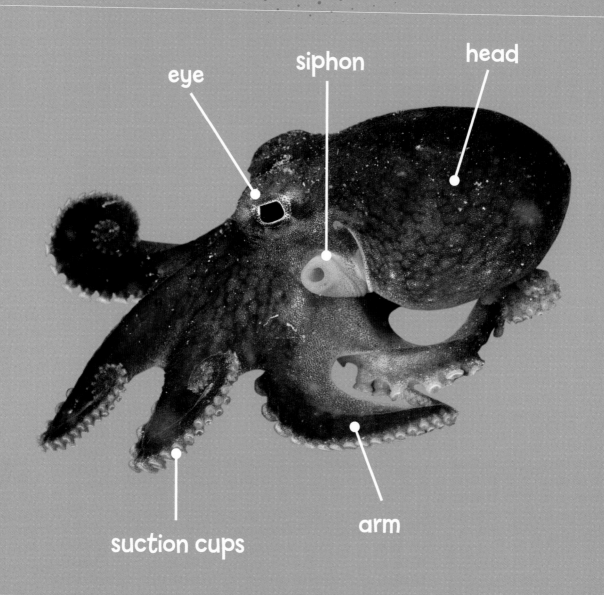

eye

siphon

head

arm

suction cups

Fun Facts

- Octopuses that live in shallow water have been seen leaping from the water to grab a crab to eat. After they grabbed their prey, they quickly got back into the water.

- Octopuses drill holes in clamshells to eat the clam inside. They use a sharp body part in their mouths to drill the holes.

- An octopus named Inky escaped from the National Aquarium of New Zealand! He climbed out of his tank, walked across the room, and squeezed into a pipe that led to the ocean.

Glossary

hatch: to break out of an egg

mate: to join together to produce young

pollution: materials that harm Earth's water, air, and land

predator: an animal that hunts and eats other animals for food

shelter: something that covers or protects

siphon: a tubelike body part. An octopus's siphon pushes water out of its body.

texture: the way that something feels when touched

Further Reading

A-Z Animals: Octopus
https://a-z-animals.com/animals/octopus/

Discovery Kids: "Octopi Have a Brain in Every Tentacle"
http://discoverykids.com/articles/octopi-have-a-brain-in-every-tentacle/

Hansen, Grace. *Octopuses*. Minneapolis: Abdo Kids, 2015.

National Geographic Kids: Octopus
http://kids.nationalgeographic.com/animals/octopus/#octopus.jpg

Pearce, Kevin. *Being an Octopus*. New York: Gareth Stevens, 2014.

Schuh, Mari. *The Supersmart Dolphin*. Minneapolis: Lerner Publications, 2019.

Index

Photo Acknowledgments

The images in this book are used with the permission of: Richard Whitcombe/Shutterstock.com, p. 2; Nature Picture Library/Getty Images, p. 4; Vladimir Wrangel/Shutterstock.com, p. 5; Pinosub/Shutterstock.com, p. 6; Placebo365/Getty Images, p. 7; SergeUWPhoto/Shutterstock.com, p. 8; Jeff Rotman/Getty Images, pp. 9, 13; Vintagepix/Shutterstock.com, p. 10; JORGEN JESSEN/AFP/Getty Images, p. 11; JonMilnes/Shutterstock.com, pp. 12, 23; Rich Carey/Shutterstock.com, p. 14; kaschibo/Shutterstock.com, p. 15; wildestanimal/Shutterstock.com, p. 16; stockphoto-graf/Shutterstock.com, p. 17; Nicram Sabod/Shutterstock.com, p. 18; l. akhundova/Shutterstock.com, p. 19; Birgitte Wilms/Minden Pictures/Getty Images, p. 20.

Cover: Andrea Izzotti/Shutterstock.com.

Main body text set in Billy Infant regular 28/36. Typeface provided by SparkType.

FEB 7 — 2019